QUEEN OF HEAVEN

PRAYERS FOR THE BATTLE

"Both St. Bernard and St. Bonaventure say that the Queen of Heaven is certainly no less grateful and conscientious than gracious and well-mannered people of this world. Just as she excels in all other perfections, she surpasses us all in the virtue of gratitude; so she would never let us honor her with love and respect without repaying us one hundredfold. St. Bonaventure says that Mary will greet us with grace if we greet her with the Hail Mary."

—Words of St. Louis De Montfort
Secret of the Rosary

QUEEN OF HEAVEN

PRAYERS FOR THE BATTLE

TAN Books
Charlotte, North Carolina

Copyright © 2017 by TAN Books.

This copyright covers this particular arrangement of existing material, plus any revisions of existing material and any other new material included herein.

Compiled from Traditional Sources.

ISBN: 978-1-5051-0999-3

Printed and bound in the United States of America.

TAN Books
Charlotte, North Carolina
www.TANBooks.com

CONTENTS

Magnificat 1
Hail Mary 2
Hail Holy Queen 2
The Memorare 2
The Angelus 3
Regina Coeli 4
Daily Offering to the Blessed Virgin Mary 5
Prayer to Mary, Mistress of the Angels 5
Sub Tuum Praesidium 6
The Woman Clothed with the Sun 6
Prayer to Mary, Help of Christians 6
Prayer of St. Aloysius Gonzaga 7
Litany of Our Lady 8
Prayer to Our Lady of Guadalupe 11
Miraculous Medal Prayer 11
Words of Our Lady of Lourdes 12
Act of Reparation to the
  Immaculate Heart Of Mary 12
Prayer to Our Lady of Lourdes 13
Novena to Our Lady of Lourdes 14
Words of Our Lady of Fatima
On Saving Souls 15
Prayer to Our Lady of Fatima 15
The Fatima Prayers 16
Words of Our Lady of Fatima on the Rosary 17

How to Pray the Rosary	18
The Mysteries of the Rosary	20
Prayers of the Rosary	21
The Five First Saturdays	24
Novena to Our Lady of Good Remedy	25
Prayer to Our Lady of Mt. Carmel	27
Novena Prayer to Our Mother of Perpetual Help	27
Prayer to Our Mother of Sorrows	28
Seven Prayers in Honor of the Seven Sorrows of the Blessed Virgin Mary	29
Mary Our Mother	33
Prayer to Our Mother of Sorrows for a Happy Death	33
A Precious Offering	34
Remember, O Virgin Mother	34
O Heart Most Pure	34
The Promises of the Seven Hail Mary's Devotion	35
Thirty Days' Prayer to the Blessed Virgin	36
Act of Total Consecration to Jesus Through Mary	40
Brief Renewal of Consecration to Jesus Through Mary	41
Short Consecration to Mary	42
My Mother, My Confidence!	42
The Seven Joys of Mary	43
The Christmas Prayer	43
The Three Hail Marys	44
Salutation to Mary	45

PRAYERS FOR THE BATTLE

MAGNIFICAT

"MY SOUL doth magnify the Lord, and my spirit hath rejoiced in God my Saviour, because He hath regarded the humility of His handmaid: for behold, from henceforth all generations shall call me blessed, because He that is mighty hath done great things to me, and holy is His Name. And His mercy is from generation unto generations, to them that fear Him.

"He hath showed might in His arm: He hath scattered the proud in the conceit of their heart. He hath put down the mighty from their seat, and hath exalted the humble. He hath filled the hungry with good things, and the rich He hath sent empty away. He hath received Israel His servant, being mindful of His mercy: as He spoke to our fathers, to Abraham and to his seed forever."

—The Blessed Virgin Mary, Luke 1:46-55

HAIL MARY
The Angelic Salutation

HAIL MARY, full of grace, the Lord is with thee; blessed art thou among women, and blessed is the Fruit of thy womb, Jesus. Holy Mary, Mother of God, pray for us sinners, now and at the hour of our death. Amen.

HAIL HOLY QUEEN
Salve Regina

HAIL HOLY QUEEN, Mother of mercy, our life, our sweetness and our hope! To thee do we cry, poor banished children of Eve. To thee do we send up our sighs, mourning and weeping in this valley of tears. Turn then, most gracious advocate, thine eyes of mercy toward us. And after this our exile, show unto us the blessed Fruit of thy womb, Jesus. O clement, O loving, O sweet Virgin Mary.

V. Pray for us, O holy Mother of God,

R. That we may be made worthy of the promises of Christ.

THE MEMORARE

REMEMBER, O most gracious Virgin Mary, that never was it known that anyone who fled to thy protection, implored thy help or sought thy intercession was left

PRAYERS FOR THE BATTLE

unaided. Inspired with this confidence, I fly unto thee, O Virgin of virgins, my Mother. To thee do I come, before thee I stand, sinful and sorrowful.

O Mother of the Word Incarnate, despise not my petitions, but in thy mercy hear and answer me. Amen.

—St. Bernard of Clairvaux (d. 1153)

THE ANGELUS

The Angelus is traditionally prayed standing, in the morning (6:00 a.m.), at noon and in the evening (6:00 p.m.), throughout the year, except during Paschal Time (Easter Sunday through the evening of the Saturday preceding Trinity Sunday), when the Regina Coeli is prayed instead.

V. The Angel of the Lord declared unto Mary.

R. And she conceived of the Holy Ghost.

Hail Mary . . .

V. Behold the handmaid of the Lord.

R. Be it done unto me according to thy word.

Hail Mary . . .

V. And the Word was made Flesh. (Genuflect.)

R. And dwelt among us. (Arise.) Hail Mary . . .

V. Pray for us, O holy Mother of God,

R. That we may be made worthy of the promises of Christ.

Let Us Pray

Pour forth, we beseech Thee, O Lord, Thy grace into our hearts, that we to whom the Incarnation of Christ, Thy Son, was made known by the message of an angel, may by His Passion and Cross be brought to the glory of His Resurrection. Through the same Christ Our Lord. Amen.

REGINA COELI

This prayer is traditionally prayed standing, in the morning (6:00 a.m.), at noon and in the evening (6:00 p.m.) during Paschal Time (from Easter Sunday through the evening of the Saturday preceding Trinity Sunday) instead of the Angelus.

V. Queen of Heaven, rejoice. Alleluia.

R. For He whom thou wast worthy to bear. Alleluia.

V. Has risen as He said. Alleluia.

R. Pray for us to God. Alleluia.

V. Rejoice and be glad, O Virgin Mary. Alleluia.

R. For the Lord is truly risen. Alleluia.

Let Us Pray

O God, Who by the Resurrection of Thy Son, Our Lord Jesus Christ, hast been pleased to give joy to the whole world, grant, we beseech Thee, that through the intercession of the Virgin Mary, His Mother, we may attain the joys of eternal life. Through the same Christ Our Lord. Amen.

PRAYERS FOR THE BATTLE

DAILY OFFERING TO THE BLESSED VIRGIN MARY

MY QUEEN and my Mother, to you I offer myself without any reserve; and to give you a mark of my devotion, I consecrate to you during this day my eyes, my ears, my mouth, my heart, and my whole person. Since I belong to you, O my good Mother, preserve and defend me as your property and possession. Amen.

PRAYER TO MARY, MISTRESS OF THE ANGELS

Given by Mary to a Bernardine Sister in approximately 1937 by Our Lady.

AUGUST Queen of Heaven!
Sovereign Mistress of the angels!
Thou who from the beginning
hast received from God
the power and mission to crush the head of Satan,
we humbly beseech thee
to send thy holy Legions,
that, under thy command
and by thy power,
they may pursue the evil spirits,
encounter them on every side,
resist their bold attacks
and drive them hence into the abyss of eternal woe.
Amen.

SUB TUUM PRAESIDIUM
Under Your Protection

The Sub Tuum Praesidium (Under Your Protection) is the oldest known Marian prayer, with origins dating back to the fifth century.

WE FLY to thy patronage, O holy Mother of God;
despise not our petitions in our necessities,
but deliver us always from all dangers,
O glorious and blessed Virgin.
Amen.

THE WOMAN CLOTHED WITH THE SUN

"AND A great sign appeared in heaven: A woman clothed with the sun, and the moon under her feet, and on her head a crown of twelve stars."

—Apocalypse 12:1

PRAYER TO MARY, HELP OF CHRISTIANS

MOST HOLY Virgin Mary, Help of Christians,
how sweet it is to come to your feet
imploring your perpetual help.
If earthly mothers cease not to remember their children,

how can you, the most loving of all mothers forget me?
Grant then to me, I implore you,
your perpetual help in all my necessities,
in every sorrow, and especially in all my temptations.
I ask for your unceasing help for all who are now suffering.
Help the weak, cure the sick, convert sinners.
Grant through your intercessions many vocations to the religious life.
Obtain for us, O Mary, Help of Christians,
that having invoked you on earth we may love and eternally thank you in heaven.

PRAYER OF ST. ALOYSIUS GONZAGA

O HOLY Mary, my Mistress, into your blessed trust and special keeping, into the bosom of your tender mercy, this day, every day of my life and at the hour of my death, I commend my soul and body; to you I entrust all my hopes and consolations, all my trials and miseries, my life and the end of my life, that through your most holy intercession and your merits, all my actions may be ordered and disposed according to your will and that of your divine Son. Amen.

LITANY OF OUR LADY
The Litany of Loreto

(For public or private use)

LORD, have mercy on us.
Christ, have mercy on us.
Lord have mercy on us. Christ, hear us.
Christ, graciously hear us.
God the Father of Heaven,
Have mercy on us.
God the Son, Redeemer of the world,
Have mercy on us.
God the Holy Ghost,
Have mercy on us.
Holy Trinity, One God,
Have mercy on us.
Holy Mary, *pray for us.*
Holy Mother of God, *pray for us.*
Holy Virgin of virgins, *pray for us.*
Mother of Christ,
Mother of divine grace,
Mother most pure,
Mother most chaste,
Mother inviolate,
Mother undefiled,
Mother most amiable,
Mother most admirable,
Mother of good counsel,
Mother of our Creator,

PRAYERS FOR THE BATTLE

Mother of our Saviour,
Virgin most prudent,
Virgin most venerable,
Virgin most renowned,
Virgin most powerful,
Virgin most merciful,
Virgin most faithful,
Mirror of Justice,
Seat of Wisdom,
Cause of our Joy,
Spiritual Vessel,
Vessel of Honor,
Singular Vessel of Devotion,
Mystical Rose,
Tower of David,
Tower of Ivory,
House of Gold,
Ark of the Covenant,
Gate of Heaven,
Morning Star,
Health of the Sick,
Refuge of Sinners,
Comforter of the Afflicted,
Help of Christians,
Queen of Angels,
Queen of Patriarchs,
Queen of Prophets,
Queen of Apostles,
Queen of Martyrs,

Queen of Confessors,
Queen of Virgins,
Queen of all Saints,
Queen conceived without Original Sin,
Queen assumed into Heaven,
Queen of the Most Holy Rosary,
Queen of Peace,
Lamb of God, Who takest away the sins of the world,
Spare us, O Lord.
Lamb of God, Who takest away the sins of the world,
Graciously hear us, O Lord.
Lamb of God, Who takest away the sins of the world,
Have mercy on us.

V. Pray for us, O holy Mother of God,

R. That we may be made worthy of the promises of Christ.

Let Us Pray

Grant, we beseech Thee, O Lord God, that we Thy servants may enjoy perpetual health of mind and body, and by the glorious intercession of the Blessed Mary, ever Virgin, be delivered from present sorrow and enjoy everlasting happiness. Through Christ Our Lord. Amen.

PRAYER TO OUR LADY OF GUADALUPE

Our Lady of Guadalupe was proclaimed "Patroness of Mexico" and "Empress of the Americas" by Pope Pius XII in 1945. In 1946 Pope Pius XII proclaimed her "Patroness of the Americas." In 1999 Pope John Paul II declared that December 12, the Feast of Our Lady of Guadalupe, would be a liturgical feast for the whole continent.

Our Lady of Guadalupe is also venerated as "Patroness of the Unborn."

HOLY MARY of Guadalupe, Mystical Rose, intercede for Holy Church, protect the Sovereign Pontiff, help all those who invoke you in their necessities; and since you are the ever Virgin Mary and Mother of the True God, obtain for us from your most holy Son the grace of keeping our faith, sweet hope in the midst of the bitterness of life, burning charity, and the precious gift of final perseverance. Amen.

MIRACULOUS MEDAL PRAYER

The Miraculous Medal was revealed to St. Catherine Labouré in 1830. Our Lady's Immaculate Conception is portrayed by images that show her crushing the serpent's head under her foot—illustrating the fact that she was never under the power of Satan for one instant of her life, beginning at her very conception. Unlike the other children of Adam, her soul was always in the state of Sanctifying Grace and never bore the stain of Original Sin. We honor Our Lady's Immaculate Conception by wearing the Miraculous Medal and by praying the invocation inscribed upon it.

O MARY, conceived without sin, pray for us who have recourse to you, and for those who do not have recourse to you, especially the enemies of the Church and those recommended to you. Amen.

WORDS OF OUR LADY OF LOURDES
to St. Bernadette (1859)

"I AM the Immaculate Conception."

"Pray for poor sinners!"

"Penance!"

ACT OF REPARATION TO THE IMMACULATE HEART OF MARY

O MOST Holy Virgin Mother, we listen with grief to the complaints of your Immaculate Heart surrounded with the thorns placed therein at every moment by the blasphemies and ingratitude of ungrateful humanity. We are moved by the ardent desire of loving you as Our Mother and of promoting a true devotion to your Immaculate Heart.

We therefore kneel before you to manifest the sorrow we feel for the grievances that people cause you, and to atone by our prayers and sacrifices for the offenses with which they return your love. Obtain for them and for us the pardon of so many sins. Hasten the conversion of sinners that they may love Jesus and cease to offend the Lord, already so much offended. Turn your eyes of mercy toward us, that we may love God with all our heart on earth and enjoy Him forever in heaven. Amen.

PRAYER TO OUR LADY OF LOURDES

This prayer to Our Lady of Lourdes draws us closer to Mary and helps us remember the amazing story of what took place in France so many years ago. Think of a special need or request as you invoke her intercession.

BLESSED, most pure Virgin, you chose to manifest yourself shining with life, sweetness and beauty in the Grotto of Lourdes.

To the child St. Bernadette, you revealed yourself, saying, "I am the Immaculate Conception."

And now, Immaculate Virgin, Mother of Mercy, Healer of the Sick, Comforter of the Afflicted, you know my wants, my troubles, my sufferings. Look upon me with mercy.

Because of your appearance in the Grotto of Lourdes, it became a privileged sanctuary from which you dispense your favors. Many have obtained the cure of their infirmities, both spiritual and physical. I come, therefore, with confidence in your maternal intercession. Obtain for me, O loving Mother, this special request.

Our Lady of Lourdes, Mother of Christ, pray for me. Obtain from your Divine Son my special request if it be God's will.

Amen.

NOVENA TO OUR LADY OF LOURDES

EVER Immaculate Virgin, Mother of Mercy, Health of the Sick, Refuge of Sinners, Comfortress of the Afflicted, you know my wants, my troubles, my sufferings. Look upon me with mercy. When you appeared in the grotto of Lourdes you made it a privileged sanctuary where you dispense your favors, and where many sufferers have obtained the cure of their infirmities, both spiritual and corporal. I come, therefore, with unbounded confidence to implore your maternal intercession. My loving Mother, obtain my request. I will try to imitate your virtues so that I may one day share your company and bless you in eternity. Amen.

PRAYERS FOR THE BATTLE

WORDS OF OUR LADY OF FATIMA ON SAVING SOULS

"PRAY! Pray a great deal, and make sacrifices for sinners, for many souls go to Hell because there is no one to pray and make sacrifices for them." (August 19, 1917).

PRAYER TO OUR LADY OF FATIMA

This prayer to Our Lady of Fatima draws us closer to Mary and helps us remember the amazing story of what took place in Portugal so many years ago. Think of a special need or request as you invoke her intercession.

O MOST Holy Virgin Mary, Queen of the most holy Rosary, you were pleased to appear to the children of Fatima and reveal a glorious message.

We implore you, inspire in our hearts a fervent love for the recitation of the Rosary.

By meditating on the mysteries of the redemption that are recalled therein may we obtain the graces and virtues that we ask, through the merits of Jesus Christ, our Lord and Redeemer. Amen.

THE FATIMA PRAYERS

PARDON PRAYER

MY GOD, I believe, I adore, I hope, and I love Thee! I ask pardon for those who do not believe, do not adore, do not hope, and do not love Thee.

THE ANGEL'S PRAYER

The children of Fatima prayed this prayer over and over, bowed low, with their foreheads touching the ground.

MOST HOLY Trinity, Father, Son and Holy Ghost, I adore Thee profoundly. I offer Thee the Most Precious Body, Blood, Soul and Divinity of Jesus Christ, present in all the tabernacles of the world, in reparation for all the outrages, sacrileges and indifferences by which He Himself is offended. And through the infinite merits of His Most Sacred Heart and the Immaculate Heart of Mary, I beg of Thee the conversion of poor sinners.

BLESSED SACRAMENT PRAYER

MOST HOLY Trinity, I adore Thee! My God, my God, I love Thee in the Most Blessed Sacrament!

O MY JESUS (DECADE PRAYER)

To be said after the Glory Be following each decade of the Rosary.

MY JESUS, forgive us our sins, save us from the fires of Hell; lead all souls to Heaven, especially those who are most in need of Thy mercy.

PRAYERS FOR THE BATTLE

SACRIFICE PRAYER

Our Lady of Fatima said to the children: "Sacrifice yourselves for sinners, and say many times, especially whenever you make some sacrifice":

JESUS, I offer this for love of Thee, for the conversion of sinners, and in reparation for the sins committed against the Immaculate Heart of Mary.

WORDS OF OUR LADY OF FATIMA ON THE ROSARY

"PRAY THE Rosary every day, in order to obtain peace for the world and the end of the war." (May 13, 1917).

" . . . Continue praying the Rosary every day in honor of Our Lady of the Rosary, in order to obtain peace for the world and the end of the war, because only she can help you." (July 13, 1917).

"I am Our Lady of the Rosary. Continue to say the Rosary every day." (October 13, 1917).

HOW TO PRAY THE ROSARY

1. Make the Sign of the Cross and say The Apostles' Creed.
2. Say the Our Father.
3. Say 3 Hail Marys.
4. Say the Glory Be to the Father.
5. Announce the First Mystery; then say the Our Father.
6. Say 10 Hail Marys.
7. Say the Glory Be to the Father.
8. Say the O My Jesus.
9. Announce the Second Mystery; then say the Our Father, 10 Hail Marys, Glory Be and O My Jesus.
10. Announce the Third Mystery; then say the Our Father, 10 Hail Marys, Glory Be and O My Jesus.
11. Announce the Fourth Mystery; then say the Our Father, 10 Hail Marys, Glory Be and O My Jesus.
12. Announce the Fifth Mystery; then say the Our Father, 10 Hail Marys, Glory Be and O My Jesus.
13. Conclude by saying the Hail, Holy Queen, Prayers for the Holy Father.

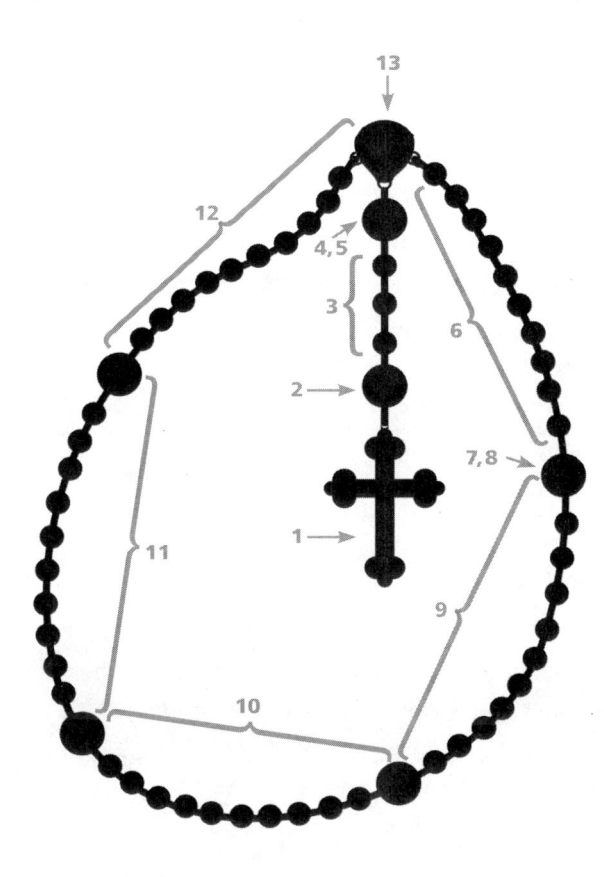

PRAYERS FOR THE BATTLE

THE MYSTERIES OF THE ROSARY

THE JOYFUL MYSTERIES

Said on Mondays and Saturdays.

1st Joyful Mystery: The Annunciation

2nd Joyful Mystery: The Visitation

3rd Joyful Mystery: The Nativity

4th Joyful Mystery: The Presentation of Our Lord in the Temple

5th Joyful Mystery: The Finding of Our Lord in the Temple

THE SORROWFUL MYSTERIES

Said on Tuesdays and Fridays.

1st Sorrowful Mystery: The Agony in the Garden

2nd Sorrowful Mystery: The Scourging at the Pillar

3rd Sorrowful Mystery: The Crowning with Thorns

4th Sorrowful Mystery: The Carrying of the Cross

5th Sorrowful Mystery: The Crucifixion and Death of Our Lord on the Cross

THE GLORIOUS MYSTERIES

Said on Wednesdays and Sundays.

1st Glorious Mystery: The Resurrection of Our Lord

2nd Glorious Mystery: The Ascension of Our Lord

PRAYERS FOR THE BATTLE

3rd Glorious Mystery: The Descent of the Holy Ghost upon the Apostles

4th Glorious Mystery: The Assumption of the Blessed Virgin Mary into Heaven

5th Glorious Mystery: The Coronation of Our Lady as Queen of Heaven and Earth

THE LUMINOUS MYSTERIES

Said on Thursdays.

1st Luminous Mystery: The Baptism in the Jordan

2nd Luminous Mystery: Our Lord's Self-manifestation at the Wedding of Cana

3rd Luminous Mystery: The proclamation of the Kingdom of God and call to conversion

4th Luminous Mystery: The Transfiguration

5th Luminous Mystery: The Institution of the Eucharist, as the sacramental expression of the Paschal Mystery

PRAYERS OF THE ROSARY

THE SIGN OF THE CROSS

IN THE NAME of the Father, and of the Son, and of the Holy Ghost. Amen.

THE APOSTLES' CREED

I BELIEVE in God, the Father Almighty, Creator of heaven and earth; and in Jesus Christ, His only Son, Our Lord; who was conceived by the Holy Ghost, born of the Virgin Mary, suffered under Pontius Pilate, was crucified, died, and was buried. He descended into hell; the third day He arose again from the dead; He ascended into Heaven, sitteth at the right hand of God, the Father Almighty; from thence He shall come to judge the living and the dead. I believe in the Holy Ghost, the Holy Catholic Church, the Communion of Saints, the forgiveness of sins, the resurrection of the body, and life everlasting. Amen.

OUR FATHER

OUR FATHER, Who art in Heaven, hallowed be Thy Name. Thy kingdom come, Thy will be done on earth as it is in Heaven. Give us this day our daily bread, and forgive us our trespasses, as we forgive those who trespass against us. And lead us not into temptation, but deliver us from evil. Amen.

HAIL MARY

HAIL MARY, full of grace, the Lord is with thee; blessed art thou among women, and blessed is the Fruit of thy womb, Jesus. Holy Mary, Mother of God, pray for us sinners, now and at the hour of our death. Amen.

PRAYERS FOR THE BATTLE

GLORY BE

GLORY BE to the Father, and to the Son, and to the Holy Ghost. As it was in the beginning, is now, and ever shall be, world without end. Amen.

O MY JESUS

MY JESUS, forgive us our sins, save us from the fires of Hell; lead all souls to Heaven, especially those who are most in need of Thy mercy.

HAIL HOLY QUEEN (SALVE REGINA)

HAIL HOLY QUEEN, Mother of mercy, our life, our sweetness and our hope! To thee do we cry, poor banished children of Eve. To thee do we send up our sighs, mourning and weeping in this valley of tears. Turn then, most gracious advocate, thine eyes of mercy toward us. And after this our exile, show unto us the blessed Fruit of thy womb, Jesus. O clement, O loving, O sweet Virgin Mary.

V. Pray for us, O holy Mother of God,

R. That we may be made worthy of the promises of Christ.

Let us pray:

GOD, Whose only-begotten Son, by His life, death and Resurrection, has purchased for us the rewards of eternal salvation, grant, we beseech Thee, that, meditating upon these Mysteries of the Most Holy Rosary of the Blessed Virgin Mary, we may both imitate what they contain and obtain what they promise.

Through the same Christ Our Lord. Amen.

THE FIVE FIRST SATURDAYS

ON JULY 13, 1917 Our Lady of Fatima said, "I shall come to ask for . . . the Communion of Reparation on the First Saturdays."

Our Lady fulfilled this promise when she and the Child Jesus appeared to Sister Lucia on December 10, 1925.

Our Lady said:

"Look, my daughter, at my heart, surrounded by thorns with which ungrateful men pierce me at every moment by their blasphemies and ingratitude. You, at least, try to console me, and announce in my name that I promise to assist at the hour of death, with all the graces necessary for salvation, all those who, on the first Saturday of five consecutive months, confess, receive Holy Communion, recite five decades of the Rosary and keep me company for fifteen minutes meditating on the fifteen mysteries of the Rosary, with the intention of making reparation to me."

On another occasion, Our Lord appeared to Sister Lucia and told her that the Confession could be made within eight days of the First Saturday, or even later on, provided that one were in the state of grace when receiving Communion and had the intention of making reparation to the Immaculate Heart of Mary. Regarding those who forget to form this intention, Our Lord answered: "They can form it at the next Confession, taking advantage of their first opportunity to go to Confession."

The 15-minute meditation does not have to cover all 15 Mysteries. Sister Lucia explained that she herself meditated on only one Mystery each First Saturday, going through the 15 Mysteries one by one and then beginning again with the Annunciation.

NOVENA TO OUR LADY OF GOOD REMEDY

QUEEN of Heaven and earth, most holy Virgin, we venerate thee. Thou art the beloved daughter of the Most High God, the chosen Mother of the Incarnate Word, the Immaculate Spouse of the Holy Spirit, the Sacred Vessel of the Most Holy Trinity. O Mother of the Divine Redeemer, who under the title of Our Lady of Good Remedy comes to the aid of all who call upon thee, extend thy maternal protection to us. We depend on thee, dear Mother, as helpless and needy children depend on a tender and caring mother.

Hail Mary . . .

O Lady of Good Remedy, source of unfailing help, grant that we may draw from thy treasury of graces in our time of need. Touch the hearts of sinners, that they may seek reconciliation and forgiveness. Bring comfort to the afflicted and the lonely; help the poor and the hopeless; aid the sick and the suffering. May they be healed in body and strengthened in spirit to endure their sufferings with patient resignation and Christian fortitude.

Hail Mary . . .

Dear Lady of Good Remedy, source of unfailing help, thy compassionate heart knows a remedy for every affliction and misery we encounter in life. Help me with thy prayers and intercession to find a remedy for my problems and needs, especially for (Indicate your special intentions here). On my part, O loving Mother, I pledge myself to a more intensely Christian lifestyle, to a more careful observance of the laws of God, to be more conscientious in fulfilling the obligations of my state in life, and to strive to be a source of healing in this broken world of ours.

Dear Lady of Good Remedy, be ever present to me, and through thy intercession, may I enjoy health of body and peace of mind, and grow stronger in the faith and in the love of thy Son, Jesus.

Hail Mary . . .

V. Pray for us, O holy Mother of Good Remedy,

R. That we may deepen our dedication to thy Son, and make the world alive with His Spirit.

Amen

PRAYER TO OUR LADY OF MT. CARMEL

(Never found to fail.)

MOST beautiful Flower of Mt. Carmel, Fruitful Vine, Splendor of Heaven, Blessed Mother of the Son of God, Immaculate Virgin, assist me in this my necessity. *(Mention your intention.)* O Star of the Sea, help me and show me in this that thou art my Mother.

O holy Mary, Mother of God, Queen of Heaven and earth, I humbly beseech thee, from the bottom of my heart, to succour me in this necessity; there are none that can withstand thy power. Oh, show me in this that thou art my Mother!

O Mary, conceived without sin, pray for us who have recourse to thee. *(three times)*

Sweet Mother, I place this cause in thy hands. *(three times)*

(It is suggested to offer three times the Our Father, Hail Mary and Glory Be in thanksgiving.)

NOVENA PRAYER TO OUR MOTHER OF PERPETUAL HELP

MOTHER of Perpetual Help, thou art the dispenser of all the gifts which God grants to us miserable sinners; and for this reason He has made thee so powerful, so rich and so bountiful, in order that thou mayest help us in our misery. Thou art the advocate of the most wretched and abandoned sinners who have recourse to thee. Come then to my aid, dearest Mother, for I recommend myself to thee. In thy hands I place my eternal salvation, and to thee do I entrust my soul. Count me among thy most devoted servants; take me under thy protection, and it is enough for me. For if thou wilt protect me, dear Mother, I fear nothing: not from my sins, because thou wilt obtain for me the pardon of them; nor from the devils, because thou art more powerful than all Hell together; nor even from Jesus, my Judge Himself, because by one prayer from thee, He will be appeased. But one thing I fear, that in the hour of temptation, I may neglect to call upon thee, and thus perish miserably.

Obtain for me, then, the pardon of my sins, love for Jesus, final perseverance, and the grace always to have recourse to thee, O Mother of Perpetual Help.

Hail Mary . . . *(three times)*

PRAYER TO OUR MOTHER OF SORROWS

This prayer to Our Mother of Sorrows, and all other novenas and prayers like it, calls to mind the profound anguish Mary endured throughout her life, especially at the foot of the Cross. We find in her a source of understanding, comfort, and strength in dealing with our own trials, for she was a woman who knew the bitter taste of human suffering and knew that we could overcome it only by having faith in her Son.

OUR MOTHER of Sorrows, with strength from above you stood by the cross, sharing in the sufferings of Jesus, and with tender care you bore Him in your arms, mourning and weeping.

We praise you for your faith, which accepted the life God planned for you. We praise you for your hope, which trusted that God would do great things in you. We praise you for your love in bearing with Jesus the sorrows of His passion.

Holy Mary, may we follow your example, and stand by all your children who need comfort and love. Mother of God, stand by us in our trials and care for us in our many needs. Pray for us now and at the hour of our death. Amen.

SEVEN PRAYERS IN HONOR OF THE SEVEN SORROWS OF THE BLESSED VIRGIN MARY

Approved by Pope Pius VII in 1815.

Begin thus:

V. O God, come to my assistance.

R. O Lord, make haste to help me.

V. Glory be to the Father, and to the Son, and to the Holy Ghost,

R. As it was in the beginning, is now, and ever shall be, world without end. Amen.

FIRST SORROW
The Prophecy of Simeon

GRIEVE for thee, O Mary most sorrowful, in the affliction of thy tender heart at the prophecy of the holy and aged Simeon. Dear Mother, by thy heart so afflicted, obtain for me the virtue of humility and the gift of the holy Fear of God.

Hail Mary . . .

SECOND SORROW
The Flight into Egypt

GRIEVE for thee, O Mary most sorrowful, in the anguish of thy most affectionate heart during the flight into Egypt and thy sojourn there. Dear Mother, by thy heart so troubled, obtain for me the virtue of generosity, especially toward the poor, and the gift of Piety.

Hail Mary . . .

THIRD SORROW
The Loss of the Child Jesus in the Temple

GRIEVE for thee, O Mary most sorrowful, in those anxieties which tried thy troubled heart at the loss of thy dear Jesus. Dear Mother, by thy heart so full of anguish, obtain for me the virtue of chastity and the

PRAYERS FOR THE BATTLE

gift of Knowledge.

Hail Mary . . .

FOURTH SORROW
Mary Meets Jesus on the Way to Calvary

GRIEVE for thee, O Mary most sorrowful, in the consternation of thy heart at meeting Jesus as He carried His cross. Dear Mother, by thy heart so troubled, obtain for me the virtue of patience and the gift of Fortitude.

Hail Mary . . .

FIFTH SORROW
Jesus Dies on the Cross

GRIEVE for thee, O Mary most sorrowful, in the martyrdom which thy generous heart endured in standing near Jesus in His agony. Dear Mother, by thy afflicted heart, obtain for me the virtue of temperance and the gift of Counsel.

Hail Mary . . .

SIXTH SORROW
Mary Receives the Dead Body of Jesus in Her Arms

GRIEVE for thee, O Mary most sorrowful, in the wounding of thy compassionate heart when the side of Jesus was struck by the lance and His heart was pierced before His body was removed from the cross.

Dear Mother, by thy heart thus transfixed, obtain for me the virtue of fraternal charity and the gift of Understanding.

Hail Mary . . .

SEVENTH SORROW
Jesus Is Placed in the Tomb

GRIEVE for thee, O Mary most sorrowful, for the pangs that wrenched thy most loving heart at the burial of Jesus. Dear Mother, by thy heart sunk in the bitterness of desolation, obtain for me the virtue of diligence and the gift of Wisdom.

Hail Mary . . .

V. Pray for us, O Virgin most sorrowful,

R. That we may be made worthy of the promises of Christ.

Let Us Pray

Let intercession be made for us, we beseech Thee, O Lord Jesus Christ, now and at the hour of our death, before the throne of Thy mercy, by the Blessed Virgin Mary, Thy Mother, whose most holy soul was pierced by a sword of sorrow in the hour of Thy bitter Passion. Through Thee, O Jesus Christ, Saviour of the world, Who with the Father and the Holy Ghost live and reign world without end. Amen.

PRAYERS FOR THE BATTLE

MARY OUR MOTHER

FROM THE Cross Our Lord looked down on His Mother Mary and His beloved disciple St. John. Jesus said to Mary: "Woman, behold thy son." Then He said to St. John: "Behold thy mother."

"And from that hour, the disciple took her to his own" (Cf. John 19:25-27).

PRAYER TO OUR MOTHER OF SORROWS FOR A HAPPY DEATH

MOTHER of Sorrows, by the anguish and love with which thou didst stand by the Cross of Jesus, stand by me in my last agony. To thy maternal heart I commend the last three hours of my life. Offer these hours to the Eternal Father in union with the agony of our dearest Lord. Offer frequently to the Eternal Father, in atonement for my sins, the Precious Blood of Jesus, mingled with thy tears on Calvary, to obtain for me the grace to receive Holy Communion with most perfect love and contrition before my death, and to breathe forth my soul in the actual presence of Jesus.

Dearest Mother, when the moment of my death has come, present me as thy child to Jesus; say to Him on my behalf: "Son, forgive him, for he knew not what he did. Receive him this day into Thy kingdom." Amen.

A PRECIOUS OFFERING

St. John Vianney, the Curé of Ars, was accustomed in special necessities to offer to the Eternal Father, by the hands of Mary, our Divine Saviour all covered with blood and wounds. This, he said, was an infallible means to obtain the most precious graces. The following words may be used to make this offering:

MARY, Mother of Sorrows, I beseech thee, by the inexpressible tortures thou didst endure at the death of thy Son, offer to the Eternal Father, in my stead, thy beloved Son all covered with blood and wounds, for the grace of (make your request). Amen.

REMEMBER, O VIRGIN MOTHER

REMEMBER, O Virgin Mother of God, when thou shalt stand before the face of the Lord, to speak favorable things in our behalf, that He may turn away His indignation from us.

O HEART MOST PURE

O HEART most pure of the Blessed Virgin Mary, obtain for me from Jesus a pure and humble heart.

THE PROMISES OF THE SEVEN HAIL MARY'S DEVOTION

According to St. Bridget of Sweden (1303-1373), the Blessed Virgin grants seven graces to those who honor her daily by saying seven Hail Marys while meditating on her tears and sorrows:

1. "I will grant peace to their families."
2. "They will be enlightened about the divine Mysteries."
3. "I will console them in their pains, and I will accompany them in their work."
4. "I will give them as much as they ask for, as long as it does not oppose the adorable Will of my Divine Son or the sanctification of their souls."
5. "I will defend them in their spiritual battles with the infernal enemy, and I will protect them at every instant of their lives."
6. "I will visibly help them at the moment of their death—they will see the face of their mother."
7. "I have obtained this grace from my Divine Son, that those who propagate this devotion to my tears and dolors will be taken directly from this earthly life to eternal happiness, since all their sins will be forgiven, and my Son will be their eternal consolation and joy."

THIRTY DAYS' PRAYER TO THE BLESSED VIRGIN

EVER GLORIOUS and blessed Mary, Queen of Virgins, Mother of Mercy, hope and comfort of dejected and desolate souls! Through that sword of sorrow which pierced thy tender heart whilst thine only Son, Christ Jesus Our Lord, suffered death and ignominy on the Cross; through that filial tenderness and pure love He had for thee, grieving at thy grief, whilst from His cross He commended thee to the care and protection of His beloved disciple St. John; take pity, I beseech thee, on my poverty and necessities; have compassion on my anxieties and cares; assist and comfort me in all my infirmities and miseries, of whatsoever kind.

Thou art the Mother of Mercies, the sweet Consolatrix and only refuge of the needy and the orphan, of the desolate and afflicted. Cast, therefore, an eye of pity on a miserable, forlorn child of Eve, and hear my prayer. For since, in just punishment of my sins, I find myself encompassed by a multitude of evils and oppressed with much anguish of spirit, whither can I fly for more secure shelter, O amiable Mother of my Lord and Saviour Jesus Christ, than under the wings of thy maternal protection? Attend, therefore, I beseech thee, with an ear of pity and compassion, to my humble and earnest request.

PRAYERS FOR THE BATTLE 37

I ask it through the bowels of mercy of thy dear Son; through that love and condescension wherewith He embraced our nature when, in compliance with the Divine Will, thou gavest thy consent, and whom, after the expiration of nine months, thou didst bring forth from the chaste enclosure of thy womb to visit this world and bless it with His presence.

I ask it through that anguish of mind wherewith thy beloved Son, our dear Saviour, was overwhelmed on Mount Olivet when He besought His Eternal Father to remove from Him, if possible, the bitter chalice of His future Passion. I ask it through the threefold repetition of His prayers in the Garden, from whence afterwards, with dolorous steps and mournful tears, thou didst accompany Him to the doleful theatre of His death and sufferings. I ask it through the welts and sores of His virginal flesh occasioned by the cords and whips wherewith He was bound and scourged when stripped of His seamless garment, for which His executioners afterwards cast lots. I ask it through the scoffs and ignominies by which He was insulted; the false accusations and unjust sentence by which He was condemned to death, and which He bore with heavenly patience. I ask it through His bitter tears and bloody sweat, His silence and resignation, His sadness and grief of heart. I ask it through the blood which trickled from His royal and sacred Head when struck with the scepter of a reed and pierced with His crown of thorns.

I ask it through the excruciating torments He suffered when His hands and feet were fastened with gross nails to the tree of the Cross. I ask it through His vehement thirst and bitter potion of vinegar and gall. I ask it through His dereliction on the Cross when He exclaimed: "My God! My God! Why hast Thou forsaken me?" I ask it through His mercy extended to the Good Thief, and through His commending His precious soul and spirit into the hands of His Eternal Father before He expired, saying: "It is consummated." I ask it through the blood mixed with water which issued from His sacred side when pierced with a lance, and whence a flood of grace and mercy has flowed to us.

I ask it through His immaculate life, bitter Passion and ignominious death on the Cross, at which nature itself was thrown into convulsions by the bursting of rocks, rending of the veil of the Temple, the earthquake, and darkness of the sun and moon. I ask it through His descent into hell, where He comforted the Saints of the Old Law with His presence and led captivity captive.

I ask it through His glorious victory over death, when He arose again to life on the third day; and through the joy which His appearance for 40 days after gave thee, His Blessed Mother, His Apostles, and the rest of His disciples, when in thine and their presence He miraculously ascended into Heaven. I ask it through

PRAYERS FOR THE BATTLE 39

the grace of the Holy Ghost infused into the hearts of His disciples when He descended upon them in the form of fiery tongues, and by which they were inspired with zeal for the conversion of the world when they went forth to preach the Gospel.

I ask it through the awful appearance of thy Son at the last dreadful day, when He shall come to judge the living and the dead, and the world by fire. I ask it through the compassion He bore thee in this life, and the ineffable joy thou didst feel at thine Assumption into Heaven, where thou art eternally absorbed in the sweet contemplation of His divine perfections. O glorious and ever blessed Virgin! Comfort the heart of thy supplicant, by obtaining for me (here mention or reflect on your lawful request, under the reservation of its being agreeable to the will of God, who sees whether it will contribute toward your spiritual good).

And as I am persuaded that my Divine Saviour doth honor thee as His beloved Mother, to whom He refuses nothing, because thou askest nothing contrary to His honor, so let me speedily experience the efficacy of thy powerful intercession, according to the tenderness of thy maternal affection and His filial loving heart, who mercifully granteth the requests and complieth with the desires of those that love and fear Him. Wherefore, O most blessed Virgin, besides the object of my present petition, and whatever else I may stand in need of, obtain for me also of thy dear Son,

Our Lord and our God, a lively faith, firm hope, perfect charity, true contrition of heart, unfeigned tears of compunction, sincere confession, worthy satisfaction, abstinence from sin, love of God and my neighbor, contempt of the world, patience to suffer affronts and ignominies, nay, even, if necessary, an opprobrious death itself, for love of thy Son, our Saviour Jesus Christ. Obtain likewise for me, O sacred Mother of God, perseverance in good works, performance of good resolutions, mortification of self will, a pious conversation through life, and, at my last moments, strong and sincere repentance, accompanied by such a lively and attentive presence of mind as may enable me to receive the Last Sacraments of the Church worthily and die in thy friendship and favor.

Lastly, obtain through thy Son, I beseech thee, for the souls of my parents, brethren, relatives and benefactors, both living and dead, life everlasting, from the only Giver of every good and perfect gift, the Lord God Almighty: to whom be all power, now and forever. Amen.

ACT OF TOTAL CONSECRATION TO JESUS THROUGH MARY

These two paragraphs are the heart of the 8-paragraph Act of Total Consecration to Jesus through Mary as taught by St. Louis De Montfort. This Act is not simply a prayer; it is a

PRAYERS FOR THE BATTLE

commitment. The Act of Total Consecration is usually made after a preparation of 30 days as explained in the book True Devotion to Mary, *by St. Louis De Montfort. The Act begins by addressing Jesus, but the following two paragraphs are addressed to Mary Immaculate.*

I, (NAME), a faithless sinner, renew and ratify today in thy hands the vows of my Baptism; I renounce forever Satan, his pomps and works; and I give myself entirely to Jesus Christ, the Incarnate Wisdom, to carry my cross after Him all the days of my life, and to be more faithful to Him than I have ever been before.

In the presence of all the heavenly court I choose thee this day for my Mother and Mistress. I deliver and consecrate to thee, as thy slave, my body and soul, my goods, both interior and exterior, and even the value of all my good actions, past, present and future; leaving to thee the entire and full right of disposing of me, and all that belongs to me, without exception, according to thy good pleasure, for the greater glory of God, in time and in eternity.

BRIEF RENEWAL OF CONSECRATION TO JESUS THROUGH MARY

St. Louis De Montfort recommends the following brief act of consecration as a monthly or even daily renewal of the Consecration to Jesus through Mary for those who have made this Consecration—which is explained in his book entitled *True Devotion to Mary.*

I AM ALL THINE, and all that I have belongs to Thee, O my sweet Jesus, through Mary, Thy holy Mother.

SHORT CONSECRATION TO MARY

By St. Alphonsus Liguori

HOLY MARY, my Mistress, into thy blessed trust and special keeping, into the bosom of thy tender mercy, I commend my soul and my body this day, every day of my life and at the hour of my death. To thee I entrust all my hopes and consolations, all my trials and miseries, my life and the end of my life, that through thy most holy intercession and thy merits, all my actions may be ordered and disposed according to thy will and that of thy Divine Son. Amen.

MY MOTHER, MY CONFIDENCE!
Mater Mea, Fiducia Mea!

O MARY Immaculate, the precious name of Mother of Confidence, with which we honor thee, fills our hearts to overflowing with the sweetest consolation and moves us to hope for every blessing from thee. If such a title has been given to thee, it is a sure sign that no one has recourse to thee in vain. Accept, therefore, with a mother's love, our devout homage, as we earnestly beseech thee to be gracious unto us in our every need. Above all do we pray thee to make us live in constant union with thee and thy Divine Son, Jesus. With thee as our guide, we are certain that we shall ever walk in the right way, in such wise that it will be our happy lot to hear thee say on the last day of our life those words of comfort: "Come then, my good and faithful servant; enter thou into the joy of thy Lord." Amen.

My Mother, my Confidence!

THE SEVEN JOYS OF MARY

As listed in the Franciscan Crown.

1. The Annunciation
2. The Visitation
3. The Nativity
4. The Adoration by the Magi
5. The Finding of Our Lord in the Temple
6. The Resurrection
7. The Assumption and Coronation of Our Lady

THE CHRISTMAS PRAYER

It is piously believed that whoever recites this prayer fifteen times a day from the Feast of St. Andrew (November 30) until Christmas will obtain what is asked.

HAIL AND BLESSED be the hour and the moment in which the Son of God was born of the most pure Virgin Mary at midnight, in Bethlehem, in piercing cold. In that hour vouchsafe, O my God, to hear my prayer and grant my desires, through the merits of our Saviour Jesus Christ and of His Blessed Mother. Amen.

THE THREE HAIL MARYS

This devotion, highly recommended by saints, consists of reciting the Hail Mary three times morning and evening every day of one's life, followed by this aspiration: "O Mother mine, keep me from mortal sin this day (night); O Mother mine, keep me from mortal sin forever." The Hail Marys are recited in honor of Our Lady's Immaculate Conception.

The practice of the Three Hail Marys is especially recommended for obtaining the virtue of purity.

SWEET HEART OF MARY

SWEET Heart of Mary, be my salvation.

REJOICE, O VIRGIN MARY

REJOICE, O Virgin Mary, for thou alone hast destroyed all heresies in the whole world.

JESUS, MARY AND JOSEPH

JESUS, Mary and Joseph, I give thee my heart and my soul.

PRAYERS FOR THE BATTLE

Jesus, Mary and Joseph, assist me in my last agony.

Jesus, Mary and Joseph, may I breathe forth my soul in peace with thee.

SALUTATION TO MARY

By St. John Eudes (17th century)

A copy of this prayer was reportedly found in a book belonging to St. Margaret Mary after her death and was zealously propagated by Father Paul of Moll, O.S.B. (Belgium), 1824-1896.

HAIL MARY, Daughter of God the Father!

Hail Mary, Mother of God the Son!

Hail Mary, Spouse of God the Holy Ghost!

Hail Mary, Temple of the Most Blessed Trinity!

Hail Mary, Pure Lily of the Effulgent Trinity!

Hail Mary, Celestial Rose of the ineffable Love of God!

Hail Mary, Virgin pure and humble, of whom the King of Heaven willed to be born and with thy milk to be nourished!

Hail Mary, Virgin of Virgins!

Hail Mary, Queen of Martyrs, whose soul a sword transfixed!

Hail Mary, Lady most blessed, unto whom all power in Heaven and earth is given!

Hail Mary, My Queen and my Mother, My Life, my Sweetness and my Hope!

Hail Mary, Mother most amiable! Hail Mary, Mother most admirable! Hail Mary, Mother of Divine Love!

Hail Mary, IMMACULATE, conceived without sin!

Hail Mary, Full of grace, the Lord is with thee!

Blessed art thou among women, and blessed is the Fruit of thy womb, JESUS!

Blessed be thy spouse, St. Joseph. Blessed be thy father, St. Joachim. Blessed be thy mother, St. Anne. Blessed be thy guardian, St. John. Blessed be thy holy angel, St. Gabriel.

Glory be to God the Father, who chose thee. Glory be to God the Son, who loved thee. Glory be to God the Holy Ghost, who espoused thee.

O Glorious Virgin Mary, may all men love and praise thee.

Holy Mary, Mother of God, pray for us and bless us, now, and at death, in the Name of JESUS, thy Divine Son!

Amen.